FINISHING LINE PRESS

www.finishinglinepress.com

Sleeping with Demons

poems by

Kaecey McCormick

Finishing Line Press
Georgetown, Kentucky

Sleeping
with Demons

ACKNOWLEDGMENTS

Versions of the following poems first appeared in these publications:

"a shadow"—*The Raw Art Review,* Summer 2021 (Honorable Mention,
Mirabai Poetry Contest)
"Meditation on the Seven"—*Boston Literary Magazine*, October 2020
"The Barn"—*Pixelated Tears* (Prolific Press 2018)

Publisher: Leah Huete de Maines
Editor: Christen Kincaid
Cover Art: Selver Učanbarlić
Author Photo: Margaret McCormick
Cover Design: Elizabeth Maines McCleavy

Order online: www.finishinglinepress.com
also available on amazon.com

Author inquiries and mail orders:
Finishing Line Press
PO Box 1626
Georgetown, Kentucky 40324
USA

Table of Contents

For those who hear demons.
You are not alone.

Poet's Note

In this collection of poems, I examine the intersection of mental health and the female different personas, forms, and styles to explore loss, betrayal, violence, mood disturbances, the generational transmission of dysfunction, and more.

a shadow

something both there   and not there
an interruption of light, an echo [silent]
a place to hide, store secrets   escape

i had a cat named shadow once
not silent that cat could talk [complain]
though he did manage to hide [away]
every night when mother called him in

he ran into the street when i was seven
we found his tail   a block away [echo]

in a dream, a man with hands and a face
shrouded in darkness in ebonies in grays
told me you were but a shadow [now]
something both there   and not there
an interruption of life, an echo [silent]

maybe i'm a shadow to you [specter]
as you gaze at me from the other side

when i woke, i could see the outline
of where the man stood, hands on my
shoulders [maybe], hot breath on my face
the wake in the air after someone leaves

something both there   and not there

the barn

you enter that space
where nothing can follow
not even dreams

and breathe deep the dry air
until you reach the place
where the light falls

from two panes and shadows
flicker across the floor
covered in cast-off cigarette packs

in the spot where you once
stood on the threshold of being a girl
and being a woman

and there you stop
and listen for her voice or
watch for the flowers on her skirt

Burying the Girl

As the machine groans
the casket into the ground
he sneaks a cigarette—
a cupped hand, a quick inhale,
turning with the wind
to blow the smoke away.

It works a slow dance
over the open grave.

I catch his eye and he freezes
then shrugs as if to say
it's all too much—
this is the best I can do.

With my eyes shut I, too, inhale
to breathe in the fading vapors
and hold the remnants
in the caverns of my chest.

Grave Robbing

In the cold November wind
sticks from the barren oak tree
decorate your mossy grave,
the vases on your lonely headstone
empty as I watch them—
the people across the yard,
shouldering each other's pain.
Here I am, again empty-handed
yet there are roses and lilies
and pink carnations
and a small orange pumpkin
on the tomb of a young soldier
dead now thirty years but
someone loves him still.
If the things on their stones
are more for us than them
what harm, I wonder, at borrowing
from the dead to satisfy
my guilty, empty hands?
Ironic that in the cold gray light,
surrounded by rotting hearts
and dead unmoving eyes,
the thrill of stealing flowers
and one small orange pumpkin
makes me feel more alive.
I hope you can't see me
yet I imagine us together,
how we would have laughed
as we crept with stolen bounty
heads close, shushing each other
lest we wake the dead
lest we wake each other.
It's enough for me to set down
stolen flowers where your heart,
if there's anything left of it, lies
place the pumpkin by the shells of your eyes
and whisper words unheard against the cold
November wind to a box covered in angels
and filled with empty promises.

In Autumn

The old woman walking down the street hugs
the inside edge of the sidewalk, her practical shoes snapping
and crunching the red and brown leaves beneath her feet
and I can tell by the way she leans from the passersby
and the traffic that her goal on these mid-morning ventures
is to simply stay alive, avoid the contamination of humans,
the flattening effect of cars

Months ago when the sun blazed away the air and clouds
and no leaves littered the footpath I waved a greeting,
tried a smile, said good morning in a voice loud enough for aging ears
but she only leaned further from me and shuttered her eyes,
pinched her face in a silent revulsion that spread down her neck
and something in me cracked then hardened,
the stinging effect of rejection

Today I watch the leaves tumble from the safety of branches
to the hard world of concrete below with those snaps and crunches
that powder what once was alive to dust and debris and for a moment
I understand her reluctance to engage, her silent and steadfast
determination to stay alive for this season of elongating nights
when each morning's walk takes her closer to winter,
the insulating effect of dying.

Outsider

after "The Card Players" by Calvin Forbes

A fourth was needed so one of the three invited a friend
and I was dragged along as a spare, an extra—
in case another needed a break I could slip in and out
as quiet and quick as the preacher's son on a Saturday night.

The talk spun from children to men to the men they knew
and their laughter rang out like bells calling home the faithful
each Sunday and I was drawn in, laughing alongside them
as the moon rose higher and the bottles grew empty.

My three sisters: The first as fierce as the winds of change,
the second as fiery as a lit stick of dynamite, and the third
strong enough to hold them both back when they let it go too far.
And me—always the baby, even after so many of my own.

The four of us born in under four years, as if Mother and Daddy
were in a race to fill the house or trying to break a record
for the number of bottoms a woman could wipe clean
without taking us all to the crossroads for a better deal.

Even now, Mother's ghost holds my hand as I watch them
play, each to her own strength to beat each other but united
against the outsider, waiting for them to let me in.

little things

bother me

for example
yesterday

I held an egg in my mind
turning it over and over
under the heat of my thoughts
until the poem inside came close to hatching
when my sister called
                    and interrupted
so I set the egg aside
and when the call ended an hour later
it was too late
            the egg had grown too cold
and died
                                #
as we talked I watched
two hummingbirds
fly around two feeders
hanging against the aging fence
nestled between the bottle brush trees
where they grabbed a quick sip
                        between battles
they reminded me of fighter pilots
darting and dipping and dodging
the light reflecting their blues and greens
as they fought for dominance
                            for food

they were destroying themselves
dropping to the floor exhausted
trembling and so close to death
all for the right to claim it all even though
there was more
            than they could consume

she'd called to talk about the election
and her fears and she asked if moving
to Canada was too extreme
and was it expensive
                and were Americans allowed
and we talked about fake news and hate
and the quality of our air
and the burning world our children will inherit
and the way greed runs it all
even though there's enough
                        more than we can consume.

Imprints

My grandfather's ghost lives
under a jar on a shelf in my garage.
Though his best-by date was in the mid-1990s,
he has no expiration date—he just keeps
doling out the same half-baked ideas and made-up
facts and dirty jokes I don't understand,
so I trapped him with a sixteen-ounce mason jar
between the extra paper towels and a box of old photos.

Sometimes his voice sneaks out from under the lip
and hitches a ride on my neck, a choker hold of whispers
and grunts that leave bruises only I can see
and I have to carry it with me, a necklace of grief,
through the day until I can slip back into the dusty garage
and pry it off my skin and push it back under the jar
before the rest of him escapes.

I used to walk with him before he died,
the oldest man I knew, living or dead.
He always called me by my full name
unless he called me Harlot.

He was an old man when my father took his first breath,
an old man who plucked a girl from her future and strapped her
to his carpenter's tool belt with two nails forged
in the shape of my father and his twin.

One day when I was twelve, he snaked an arm
around my shoulder and squeezed me so hard
the air in my lungs rushed out to see the cause
but before I backed away he asked me if I wanted
to sit on his lap and earn a nickel.

My father pulled me away and said he doesn't mean it
but my grandfather licked his lips and smacked
his wolfy teeth and said, Oh yes I do, little Harlot.
Come back here and shake.

Now when his voice slides under the glass and climbs
up my arm to my throat, I imagine he's branding me
with his smoky breath and stamping the letter "H"
onto my breast, and no matter how hard I try
I can't stop thinking about that nickel.

Meditation on the Seven
in seven words, on seven lines, in seven stanzas

One (Lust)
I'm pretty sure this is an oversight,
not a sin, because who doesn't lust?
Why make sin central to our existence?
This must be a mistake in translation,
something taken out of context and dropped
on the unsuspecting faithful like a stone.

Two (Gluttony)
People love to let this one slide.
Look around if you don't believe me.
No need for faith in my words—
the evidence surrounds us in supersized truth.
Bible-thumping gluttons press my buttons. How
can you eat your cake in grace
while thousands die of starvation every day?

Three (Greed)
Just try avoiding avarice in America today.
It seems being boiled alive in oil
is a fair price for your luxury—
as long as it's the best oil
money can buy. I do my best
to ignore cupidity's claws. Tell me, how
many pairs of shoes are too many?

Four (Sloth)
I sat on the blue couch today,
as if that would make a difference.
It didn't. The boredom, the apathy, the
indolence. The refusal to do what needs
doing—they remain successful partners in crime.
I tell myself omission isn't a sin,
but lying about sinning is another sin.

Five (Wrath)

Yesterday, a driver on crowded Highway 101
wouldn't let me in, forcing me to
creep along the dirty shoulder, blinker flashing,
until someone let my car slowly sleaze
into the unending line of unmoving vehicles.
I imagined 101 ways for the asshole
to suffer and die, sealing my fate.

Six (Envy)

Since I don't care much about money,
I thought I was safe. And then
I saw the women on his screen
and it gripped me from the inside.
I've tried confession and prayer, but nothing
works to cool the flames of jealousy
and my desire to take their place.

Seven (Pride)

I tell my kids I am proud
of them, their major accomplishments, their minor
efforts. Is that wrong? I ask him.
He adjusts his collar and looks up.
I don't know if he's looking for
help from God or if my questions
annoy him, but he never answers me.

The Sex of Poetry

Have you ever read a poem and thought
yes please and thank you

a poem that hits you
in the right spot
and keeps hitting it
until you're moved with desire
to keep the poem tucked between your
sheets just in case you wake up lonely
and empty and want
to read the poem again?

Sex is like that. It's the first poem, really—
the one that brings you to life, occupies your nights,
distracts you daily, brings joy and pleasure
wipes away your pain
                         for a moment
makes you scream
yes please and thank you.

Do you ever think of the unpublished poems—
the ones you'll never have a chance to read?

These untouched poems make me think about the men
(and women) I'll never fuck or be fucked by. I think
what a shame too bad and oh well.

Writing poetry is like that because sometimes,
even with the most expensive paper
and a pen primed with perfect ink,
the words don't come out right, the sounds are
off, the volta lacking and you leave the table
disappointed, knowing it was an hour
                                        or ten minutes
you can't get back and you try to move on, think
what a shame too bad oh well
until the next poem grabs you

by the throat or balls
and comes to life beneath your skillful hands
and has you writhing and whimpering in your seat
whispering yes please and thank you.

counterpoint

after the first day of class   [89 bodies]
a woman comes up to me
dyed blonde   manicured   fit
Burberry black & tan

wanting to stand closer she waits
biding her time   face to phone
until it's just her   and me

we should grab a drink sometime
talk shop   compare notes
her breath   minty   hits my face

she tells me she's writing a book
wants input   wants mine
what time am I free   today
or next week

she's older by a decade   [at least]
maybe that's where the confidence comes from
mine leaves out the back door

later my husband tells me
she was looking to connect   in a different way
beyond poetry and prose
one that involves sweat   skin   lips   heat

I laugh   shake the image away
but the suggestion stays with me
haunts my nights   unlatches my eyes

at our next class meeting   [advanced fiction]
I finger the plaid scarf around my neck.

Betrayed

For so long I would not admit what he did. Even to myself
I thought around it. Called it the accident. The incident.
The Mistake. The Error. Miscalculation. The Gaffe.
Thought around the specific details: Hands on flesh.
On thighs. On other types of flesh. Worked to avoid
becoming a cliché, the woman scorned, angry and ugly
and all alone. I spoke of forgiveness but dreamed of a thousand
different ways to hurt him. Tit for tat. Never doing one.
Instead I wrote him into a poem and burned the ink,
dropped the ashes in the toilet and flushed away
the occurrence with his other shit. One cliché
replacing another.

American Strip Mall

"Slop has purpose. This much I know." - Lisa Gill

In my locked car, my world is contained. Manageable. Only so much baggage can fit in a hatchback, though it's more than I would have guessed. The rain blurs the outside world, the fuzzy windows insulating as I peer through the glass, like a blanket of disbelief protecting against the stab of betrayal when she steps from the car and shakes open her umbrella. I could leave them cloudy. Pretend. Hold on to some reasonable doubt. Instead, I rub my hand against the cold glass to clear the view and notice the bend of her back, the curve of her ass in tight dark jeans when she leans through the door to say goodbye. I consider leaving this parking lot next to the Home Depot, this home of Arby's and Annie's Nails and QuickE Liquors, and driving myself to the nearest psych ward so I can sleep this away. Sleep us away. What's a little shock therapy between the lobes when your world disappears? As I watch her drive away, I stare at the red lights on the back of your car and want nothing more than to watch them turn white—as if you could reverse this with one shift, spin the world backward like a superhero with the turning wheels of your car, until the baggage is unloaded and we are back at the start, bright-eyed and hopeful. But you drive forward and away, and I feel a part of me go with you. I'm stretched across the wet night, like a web pulled between trees, losing hold on both ends and sagging in the middle until instead of breaking, I let go and drift to the puddles pooling on the slick blacktop and watch myself dissolve.

Puppets

after "Pinocchios" by Clare Pollard

think of a marionette
jointed limbs flailing
head bobbing up and down
up and down
movement manipulated from above
by invisible wires
and think of all the women
the girlfriends wives mothers daughters
whole heads
bob up and down up and down
on wood and the men
watching the show as they jerk
and pull harder at the strings
held in place by babies or money or fear
or love
think of all the women who feel a hand
enter the hollow inside them turning their heads
back and forth
and think of the men finger puppets
made to jump and bounce and grate
against the slightest twist of a thumb
think of the faithful and the chosen
the true believers who
by the millions
kneel and bow and fold their arms
and open their mouths
and act out the will of an unseen
puppeteer   a force
no one can see but strong
enough to drive planes into buildings
swords through necks
nails through flesh
think of the children
clapping their hands together in song
think of Lady Elaine Fairchilde
standing up to the king
but ending up back in the neighborhood

bowing with the rest
think of a marionette resting
eyes wide open wheels spinning
unable to act until someone
tugs her strings

(un)tether

for only $1999 you can transform your eyes, get 20/20 vision
but what they don't tell you is that it only works on hindsight
when i try to look away from my past my eyes get stuck
i can't tell where to look first and i can't look away

i thought about having them move my eyes to my fingertips
so i could get a better look inside the hard-to-reach places
but that required me to give one-half of my stomach as a deposit
and they won't take the other half if what you find makes you sick

too dangerous

instead i ask you to stroke my face
and hold me while i fall asleep
then sew my eyes shut

i thought it would be better not to see at all, to be cloaked in eternal
dark
but instead of darkness behind my lids it all lights up and i'm forced
to watch
rainbows as light catches shards of glass shattered on the spanish tile
floor
rorschach patterns of blood on the lace curtains and her new winter
coat
the angle of her head before they cover it in a crisp white sheet

i know i have to get away from it so i ask you
what will they charge to cut off my head
you tell me it's easier to sever my feet

From an Empty Place

I have not come to understand
letters empty letters
or cases empty cases
where pens or pencils or tongues
should be
to be or not
to be important
to be understood
to be change
the change I want to be
to bring change
change to the letters
from empty letters to empty cases
and empty tongues.
I have changed
changed clothes changed hair
changed men changed homes
but still the empty letters
or cases empty cases
where pens or pencils or tongues
should be

rebirth

every night I re-enter the womb,
curl into a kidney bean, tight and small
twist six feet of limbs around my shell
a mess of shoulders and backbone and skull
and wrap myself in the warm, dark shelter
and hold my breath, waiting for it to come

every night I'm unwrapped, piece by piece,
a hand stinging across my skin like wildfire,
slapped awake and stretched and pulled open
then filled and rubbed and pressed and pounded
over and over and again and again until I'm left,
exposed, naked and bloody on clean white sheets
watched under a single bright light

i am the river birch

white bark rips and peels, layer by layer
like mica flakes stripping down the years
revealing naked petal-smooth skin, trapped
under my fingertips life, wet and warm

like mica flakes stripping down the years
like lovers tearing off clothes, piece by piece
under my fingertips life, wet and warm
under my skin, shadows sag and fall

like lovers tearing off clothes, piece by piece
i remove my head and pull my veins to look inside
under my skin, shadows sag and fall
and my fingers break apart at the joints to bleed

i remove my head and pull my veins to look inside
white bark rips and peels, layer by layer
and my fingers break apart at the joints to bleed
revealing naked petal-smooth skin, trapped

Sleeping with Demons

I cradle the awl and watch
as the hole in my chest
widens until it sucks me
into the darkness
I crawl through the black
drag what's left of my body
bumping into unseen walls
barriers to the light
my blinded eyes seek
but only cold shadows
echoes of sanity
trace my skin in the mist
teasing, taunting me
with their nearness
even as they slip
from my reach
I struggle to wake
stand on twisted feet,
fighting
sink my shaking hands
deeper into the slick opening
in the middle of my chest
press my fingers through the sinew
and savor the warmth of blood
on my cold skin as I squeeze.

Kaecey McCormick is a writer living in the San Francisco Bay Area. Her poetry and prose have found homes in different places, including *Pine Hills Review, Jabberwock Review, One Sentence Poems, On the Seawall, Third Wednesday* and *Clockhouse* as well as her first chapbook, *Pixelated Tears* (2018). She served as poet laureate for the city of Cupertino, teaches poetry at The Writers Studio, and is a current Steinbeck Fellow at SJSU. When not writing, you can find Kaecey hiking up a mountain, painting, or reading a book. Connect at kaeceymccormick.com.